THE POST OFFICE

BY

RABINDRANATH TAGORE

TRANSLATED BY

DEVABRATA MUKERJEA

MACMILLAN AND CO., LIMITED
ST. MARTIN'S STREET, LONDON
1914

THE POST OFFICE

MACMILLAN AND CO., Limited
LONDON · BOMBAY · CALCUTTA
MELBOURNE

THE MACMILLAN COMPANY
NEW YORK · BOSTON · CHICAGO
DALLAS · SAN FRANCISCO

THE MACMILLAN CO. OF CANADA, Ltd.
TORONTO

PREFACE

WHEN this little play was performed in London a year ago by the Irish players, some friends of mine discovered much detailed allegory, the Headman being one principle of social life, the Curdseller or the Gaffer another; but the meaning is less intellectual, more emotional and simple. The deliverance sought and won by the dying child is the same deliverance which rose before his imagination, Mr. Tagore has said, when once in the early dawn he heard, amid the noise of a crowd returning from some festival, this line out of an old village song, "Ferryman, take me to the other shore of the river." It may come at any moment of life, though the child discovers it in death, for it always comes at the moment when the " I," seeking no longer for gains that cannot be " assimilated with its spirit," is able to say, " All my work is thine " (*Sadhanā*, pp. 162, 163). On the stage the little play shows that it is very perfectly constructed, and conveys to the right audience an emotion of gentleness and peace.

W. B. YEATS.

THE POST OFFICE
ACT I

B

ACT I

(Madhav's House.)

Madhav

What a state I am in ! Before he came, nothing mattered ; I felt so free. But now that he has come, goodness knows from where, my heart is filled with his dear self, and my home will be no home to me when he leaves. Doctor, do you think he——

Physician

If there's life in his fate, then he will live long. But what the medical scriptures say, it seems——

Madhav

Great heavens, what ?

Physician

The scriptures have it : " Bile or palsey, cold or gout spring all alike."

Madhav

Oh, get along, don't fling your scriptures at me ; you only make me more anxious ; tell me what I can do.

Physician (taking snuff)

The patient needs the most scrupulous care.

Madhav

That's true ; but tell me how.

Physician

I have already mentioned, on no account must he be let out of doors.

Madhav

Poor child, it is very hard to keep him indoors all day long.

Physician

What else can you do ? The autumn sun and the damp are both very bad for the little fellow—for the scriptures have it :

" In wheezing, swooning or in nervous
    fret,
    In jaundice or leaden eyes—— "

Madhav

Never mind the scriptures, please. Eh, then we must shut the poor thing up. Is there no other method ?

Physician

None at all : for, " In the wind and in the sun—— "

Madhav

What will your " in this and in that " do for me now ? Why don't you let them alone and come straight to the point ? What's to be done

then? Your system is very, very
hard for the poor boy; and he is so
quiet too with all his pain and sick-
ness. It tears my heart to see him
wince, as he takes your medicine.

Physician

The more he winces, the surer is the
effect. That's why the sage Chyabana
observes : " In medicine as in good
advice, the least palatable is the
truest." Ah, well! I must be trot-
ting now.   [*Exit.*

(*Gaffer enters.*)

Madhav

Well, I'm jiggered, there's Gaffer
now.

Gaffer

Why, why, I won't bite you.

Madhav

No, but you are a devil to send
children off their heads.

Gaffer

But you aren't a child, and you've no child in the house; why worry then ?

Madhav

Oh, but I have brought a child into the house.

Gaffer

Indeed, how so ?

Madhav

You remember how my wife was dying to adopt a child ?

Gaffer

Yes, but that's an old story; you didn't like the idea.

Madhav

You know, brother, how hard all this getting money in has been. That somebody else's child would sail in

and waste all this money earned with
so much trouble—Oh, I hated the
idea. But this boy clings to my heart
in such a queer sort of way——

Gaffer

So that's the trouble! and your
money goes all for him and feels jolly
lucky it does go at all.

Madhav

Formerly, earning was a sort of
passion with me; I simply couldn't
help working for money. Now, I
make money, and as I know it is all
for this dear boy, earning becomes a
joy to me.

Gaffer

Ah, well, and where did you pick
him up?

Madhav

He is the son of a man who was a
brother to my wife by village ties.

He has had no mother since infancy ;
and now the other day he lost his
father as well.

Gaffer

Poor thing : and so he needs me all
the more.

Madhav

The doctor says all the organs of
his little body are at loggerheads with
each other, and there isn't much hope
for his life. There is only one way
to save him and that is to keep him
out of this autumn wind and sun.
But you are such a terror ! What
with this game of yours at your age,
too, to get children out of doors !

Gaffer

God bless my soul ! So I'm already
as bad as autumn wind and sun, eh !
But, friend, I know something, too,
of the game of keeping them indoors.

When my day's work is over I am coming in to make friends with this child of yours. [*Exit.*

(*Amal enters.*)

Amal

Uncle, I say, Uncle !

Madhav

Hullo ! Is that you, Amal ?

Amal

Mayn't I be out of the courtyard at all ?

Madhav

No, my dear, no.

Amal

See, there where Auntie grinds lentils in the quirn, the squirrel is sitting with his tail up and with his wee hands he's picking up the broken

grains of lentils and crunching them.
Can't I run up there ?

Madhav

No, my darling, no.

Amal

Wish I were a squirrel !—it would
be lovely. Uncle, why won't you let
me go about ?

Madhav

Doctor says it's bad for you to be
out.

Amal

How can the doctor know ?

Madhav

What a thing to say ! The doctor
can't know and he reads such huge
books !

Amal

Does his book‑learning tell him
everything ?

Madhav

Of course, don't you know !

Amal (with a sigh)

Ah, I am so stupid ! I don't read
books.

Madhav

Now, think of it ; very, very learned
people are all like you ; they are never
out of doors.

Amal

Aren't they really ?

Madhav

No, how can they ? Early and late
they toil and moil at their books, and
they've eyes for nothing else. Now,
my little man, you are going to be

learned when you grow up ; and then
you will stay at home and read such
big books, and people will notice you
and say, " He's a wonder."

Amal

No, no, Uncle ; I beg of you by
your dear feet—I don't want to be
learned, I won't.

Madhav

Dear, dear ; it would have been my
saving if I could have been learned.

Amal

No, I would rather go about and see
everything that there is.

Madhav

Listen to that ! See ! What will
you see, what is there so much to see?

Amal

See that far-away hill from our window—I often long to go beyond those hills and right away.

Madhav

Oh, you silly ! As if there's nothing more to be done but just get up to the top of that hill and away ! Eh ! You don't talk sense, my boy. Now listen, since that hill stands there upright as a barrier, it means you can't get beyond it. Else, what was the use in heaping up so many large stones to make such a big affair of it, eh !

Amal

Uncle, do you think it is meant to prevent us crossing over ? It seems to me because the earth can't speak it raises its hands into the sky and beckons. And those who live far off, and sit alone by their windows can see

the signal. But I suppose the learned
people——

Madhav

No, they don't have time for that
sort of nonsense. They are not crazy
like you.

Amal

Do you know, yesterday I met
some one quite as crazy as I am.

Madhav

Gracious me, really, how so ?

Amal

He had a bamboo staff on his
shoulder with a small bundle at the
top, and a brass pot in his left hand,
and an old pair of shoes on; he was
making for those hills straight across
that meadow there. I called out to
him and asked, "Where are you
going ? " He answered, " I don't

know, anywhere!" I asked again,
"Why are you going?" He said,
"I'm going out to seek work." Say,
Uncle, have you to seek work?

Madhav

Of course I have to. There's many
about looking for jobs.

Amal

How lovely! I'll go about, like
them too, finding things to do.

Madhav

Suppose you seek and don't find.
Then——

Amal

Wouldn't that be jolly? Then I
should go farther! I watched that
man slowly walking on with his pair
of worn-out shoes. And when he got
to where the water flows under the

fig tree, he stopped and washed his
feet in the stream.   Then he took out
from his bundle some gram - flour,
moistened it with water and began to
eat.   Then he tied up his bundle and
shouldered it again; tucked up his
cloth above his knees and crossed the
stream.   I've asked Auntie to let me
go up to the stream, and eat my
gram-flour just like him.

Madhav

And what did your Auntie say to
that ?

Amal

Auntie said, " Get well and then I'll
take you over there."   Please, Uncle,
when shall I get well ?

Madhav

It won't be long, dear.

c

Amal

Really, but then I shall go right away the moment I'm well again.

Madhav

And where will you go ?

Amal

Oh, I will walk on, crossing so many streams, wading through water. Everybody will be asleep with their doors shut in the heat of the day and I will tramp on and on seeking work far, very far.

Madhav

I see ! I think you had better be getting well first ; then——

Amal

But then you won't want me to be learned, will you, Uncle?

Madhav

What would you rather be then ?

Amal

I can't think of anything just now ;
but I'll tell you later on.

Madhav

Very well. But mind you, you
aren't to call out and talk to strangers
again.

Amal

But I love to talk to strangers !

Madhav

Suppose they had kidnapped you ?

Amal

That would have been splendid !
But no one ever takes me away.
They all want me to stay in here.

Madhav

I am off to my work—but, darling,
you won't go out, will you ?

Amal

No, I won't.   But, Uncle, you'll let
me be in this room by the roadside.
                    [*Exit Madhav.*

Dairyman

Curds, curds, good nice curds.

Amal

Curdseller, I say, Curdseller.

Dairyman

Why do you call me ?   Will you
buy some curds ?

Amal

How can I buy ?   I have no money.

Dairyman

What a boy! Why call out then?
Ugh! What a waste of time.

Amal

I would go with you if I could.

Dairyman

With me?

Amal

Yes, I seem to feel homesick when
I hear you call from far down the
road.

Dairyman (lowering his yoke-pole)

Whatever are you doing here, my
child?

Amal

The doctor says I'm not to be out,
so I sit here all day long.

Dairyman

My poor child, whatever has happened to you ?

Amal

I can't tell. You see I am not learned, so I don't know what's the matter with me. Say, Dairyman, where do you come from ?

Dairyman

From our village.

Amal

Your village ?   Is it very far ?

Dairyman

Our village lies on the river Shamli at the foot of the Panch-mura hills.

Amal

Panch-mura hills ! Shamli river ! I wonder. I may have seen your village. I can't think when though !

Dairyman

Have you seen it ? Been to the
foot of those hills ?

Amal

Never. But I seem to remember
having seen it. Your village is under
some very old big trees, just by the
side of the red road—isn't that so ?

Dairyman

That's right, child.

Amal

And on the slope of the hill cattle
grazing.

Dairyman

How wonderful ! Cattle grazing in
our village ! Indeed, there are !

Amal

And your women with red sarees fill their pitchers from the river and carry them on their heads.

Dairyman

Good, that's right. Women from our dairy village do come and draw their water from the river; but then it isn't every one who has a red saree to put on. But, my dear child, surely you must have been there for a walk some time.

Amal

Really, Dairyman, never been there at all. But the first day doctor lets me go out, you are going to take me to your village.

Dairyman

I will, my child, with pleasure.

Amal

And you'll teach me to cry curds and shoulder the yoke like you and walk the long, long road ?

Dairyman

Dear, dear, did you ever ? Why should you sell curds ? No, you will read big books and be learned.

Amal

No, I never want to be learned—I'll be like you and take my curds from the village by the red road near the old banyan tree, and I will hawk it from cottage to cottage. Oh, how do you cry—" Curds, curds, fine curds ! " Teach me the tune, will you ?

Dairyman

Dear, dear, teach you the tune; what a notion !

Amal

Please do. I love to hear it. I can't tell you how queer I feel when I hear you cry out from the bend of that road, through the line of those trees ! Do you know I feel like that when I hear the shrill cry of kites from almost the end of the sky ?

Dairyman

Dear child, will you have some curds ? Yes, do.

Amal

But I have no money.

Dairyman

No, no, no, don't talk of money ! You'll make me so happy if you take some curds from me.

Amal

Say, have I kept you too long ?

Dairyman

Not a bit; it has been no loss to me at all; you have taught me how to be happy selling curds.   [*Exit.*

Amal (*intoning*)

Curds, curds, fine curds—from the dairy village—from the country of the Panch-mura hills by the Shamli bank. Curds, good curds; in the early morning the women make the cows stand in a row under the trees and milk them, and in the evening they turn the milk into curds. Curds, good curds. Hello, there's the watchman on his rounds. Watchman, I say, come and have a word with me.

Watchman

What's all this row about ? Aren't you afraid of the likes of me ?

Amal

No, why should I be ?

Watchman

Suppose I march you off then ?

Amal

Where will you take me to ?   Is it very far, right beyond the hills ?

Watchman

Suppose I march you straight to the King ?

Amal

To the King !   Do, will you ?   But the doctor won't let me go out.   No one can ever take me away.   I've got to stay here all day long.

Watchman

Doctor won't let you, poor fellow ! So I see !   Your face is pale and there are dark rings round your eyes.   Your veins stick out from your poor thin hands.

Amal

Won't you sound the gong, Watchman ?

Watchman

Time has not yet come.

Amal

How curious ! Some say time has
not yet come, and some say time has
gone by ! But surely your time will
come the moment you strike the
gong !

Watchman

That's not possible ; I strike up the
gong only when it is time.

Amal

Yes, I love to hear your gong.
When it is mid-day and our meal is
over, Uncle goes off to his work and
Auntie falls asleep reading her Ramayana, and in the courtyard under the

shadow of the wall our doggie sleeps with his nose in his curled - up tail; then your gong strikes out, " Dong, dong, dong ! " Tell me why does your gong sound ?

Watchman

My gong sounds to tell the people, Time waits for none, but goes on for ever.

Amal

Where, to what land ?

Watchman

That none knows.

Amal

Then I suppose no one has ever been there ! Oh, I do wish to fly with the time to that land of which no one knows anything.

Watchman

All of us have to get there one day, my child.

Amal

Have I too ?

Watchman

Yes, you too !

Amal

But doctor won't let me out.

Watchman

One day the doctor himself may take you there by the hand.

Amal

He won't; you don't know him. He only keeps me in.

Watchman

One greater than he comes and lets us free.

Amal

When will this great doctor come for me ? I can't stick in here any more.

Watchman

Shouldn't talk like that, my child.

Amal

No. I am here where they have left me—I never move a bit. But when your gong goes off, dong, dong, dong, it goes to my heart. Say, Watchman ?

Watchman

Yes, my dear.

Amal

Say, what's going on there in that big house on the other side, where

there is a flag flying high up and the
people are always going in and out ?

Watchman

Oh, there ?   That's our new Post
Office.

Amal

Post Office ? Whose ?

Watchman

Whose ?   Why, the King's surely !

Amal

Do letters come from the King to
his office here ?

Watchman

Of course.   One fine day there may
be a letter for you in there.

Amal

A letter for me ? But I am only a
little boy.

D

Watchman

The King sends tiny notes to little boys.

Amal

Oh, how splendid! When shall I have my letter? How do you know he'll write to me?

Watchman

Otherwise why should he set his Post Office here right in front of your open window, with the golden flag flying?

Amal

But who will fetch me my King's letter when it comes?

Watchman

The King has many postmen. Don't you see them run about with round gilt badges on their chests?

Amal

Well, where do they go ?

Watchman

Oh, from door to door, all through the country.

Amal

I'll be the King's postman when I grow up.

Watchman

Ha ! ha ! Postman, indeed ! Rain or shine, rich or poor, from house to house delivering letters—that's very great work !

Amal

That's what I'd like best. What makes you smile so ? Oh, yes, your work is great too. When it is silent everywhere in the heat of the noonday, your gong sounds, Dong, dong, dong,—and sometimes when I wake

up at night all of a sudden and find
our lamp blown out, I can hear through
the darkness your gong slowly sounding, Dong, dong, dong !

Watchman

There's the village headman ! I
must be off. If he catches me gossip-
ing there'll be a great to-do.

Amal

The headman ? Whereabouts is
he ?

Watchman

Right down the road there ; see
that huge palm-leaf umbrella hopping
along ? That's him !

Amal

I suppose the King's made him. our
headman here ?

Watchman

Made him? Oh, no! A fussy busybody! He knows so many ways of making himself unpleasant that everybody is afraid of him. It's just a game for the likes of him, making trouble for everybody. I must be off now! Mustn't keep work waiting, you know! I'll drop in again to-morrow morning and tell you all the news of the town. [*Exit.*

Amal

It would be splendid to have a letter from the King every day. I'll read them at the window. But, oh! I can't read writing. Who'll read them out to me, I wonder! Auntie reads her Ramayana; she may know the King's writing. If no one will, then I must keep them carefully and read them when I'm grown up. But if the postman can't find me?

Headman, Mr. Headman, may I have a word with you ?

Headman
Who is yelling after me on the highway ?   Oh it's you, is it, you wretched monkey ?

Amal
You're the headman.   Everybody minds you.

Headman (*looking pleased*)
Yes, oh yes, they do !   They must !

Amal
Do the King's postmen listen to you ?

Headman
They've got to.   By Jove, I'd like to see——

Amal
Will you tell the postman it's Amal who sits by the window here ?

Headman

What's the good of that ?

Amal

In case there's a letter for me.

Headman

A letter for you ! Whoever's going
to write to you ?

Amal

If the King does.

Headman

Ha ! ha ! What an uncommon
little fellow you are ! Ha ! ha ! the
King indeed, aren't you his bosom
friend, eh ! You haven't met for a
long while and the King is pining for
you, I am sure. Wait till to-morrow
and you'll have your letter.

Amal

Say, Headman, why do you speak
to me in that tone of voice ? Are
you cross ?

Headman

Upon my word !   Cross, indeed !
You write to the King !   Madhav is a
devilish swell nowadays.   He's made a
little pile ; and so kings and padishahs
are everyday talk with his people.
Let me find him once and I'll make
him dance.   Oh you, — you snipper-
snapper !   I'll get the King's letter
sent to your house—indeed I will !

Amal

No, no, please don't trouble yourself about it.

Headman

And why not, pray !   I'll tell the
King about you and he won't be

long.   One of his footmen will come
presently for news of you.   Madhav's
impudence staggers me.   If the King
hears of this, that'll take some of
his nonsense out of him.   [*Exit.*

Amal

Who are you walking there ?   How
your anklets tinkle !   Do stop a while,
won't you ?

(*A Girl enters.*)

Girl

I haven't a moment to spare ; it is
already late !

Amal

I see, you don't wish to stop ; I
don't care to stay on here either.

Girl

You make me think of some late
star of the morning !   Whatever's the
matter with you ?

Amal

I don't know ; the doctor won't let
me out.

Girl

Ah me ! Don't go then ! Should
listen to the doctor. People will be
cross with you if you're naughty. I
know, always looking out and watching
must make you feel tired. Let me
close the window a bit for you.

Amal

No, don't, only this one's open !
All the others are shut. But will you
tell me who you are ? Don't seem to
know you.

Girl

I am Sudha.

Amal

What Sudha ?

Sudha

Don't you know ?   Daughter of the flower-seller here.

Amal

What do *you* do ?

Sudha

I gather flowers in my basket.

Amal

Oh, flower gathering !   That is why your feet seem so glad and your anklets jingle so merrily as you walk. Wish I could be out too.   Then I would pick some flowers for you from the very topmost branches right out of sight.

Sudha

Would you really ?   Do you know as much about flowers as I ?

Amal

Yes, I *do*, quite as much. I know all about Champa of the fairy tale and his seven brothers. If only they let me, I'll go right into the dense forest where you can't find your way. And where the honey-sipping humming-bird rocks himself on the end of the thinnest branch, I will blossom into a champa. Would you be my sister Parul ?

Sudha

You are silly ! How can I be sister Parul when I am Sudha and my mother is Sasi, the flower-seller ? I have to weave so many garlands a day. It would be jolly if I could lounge here like you !

Amal

What would you do then, all the day long ?

Sudha

I could have great times with my doll Benay the bride, and Meni the pussy-cat, and—but I say, it is getting late and I mustn't stop, or I won't find a single flower.

Amal

Oh, wait a little longer; I do like it so !

Sudha

Ah, well—now don't you be naughty. Be good and sit still, and on my way back home with the flowers I'll come and talk with you.

Amal

And you'll let me have a flower then ?

Sudha

No, how can I ? It has to be paid for.

Amal

I'll pay when I grow up—before I leave to look for work out on the other side of that stream there.

Sudha

Very well, then.

Amal

And you'll come back when you have your flowers ?

Sudha

I will.

Amal

You will, really ?

Sudha

Yes, I will.

Amal

You won't forget me ?   I am Amal,
remember that.

Sudha

I won't forget you, you'll see.

[*Exit.*

(*A Troop of Boys enter.*)

Amal

Say, brothers, where are you all off
to ?   Stop here a little.

A Boy

We're off to play.

Amal

What will you play at, brothers ?

A Boy

We'll play at being ploughmen.

Another Boy (*showing a stick*)

This is our ploughshare.

Another Boy

We two are the pair of oxen.

Amal

And you're going to play the whole day ?

A Boy

Yes, all day long.

Amal

And you will come home in the evening by the road along the river bank ?

A Boy

Yes.

Amal

Do you pass our house on your way home ?

A Boy

Come out and play with us, yes
do.

Amal

Doctor won't let me out.

A Boy

Doctor ! Do you mean to say you
mind what the doctor says ? Let's be
off; it is getting late.

Amal

Don't go. Play on the road near
this window ? I could watch you
then.

A Boy

What can we play at here ?

Amal

With all these toys of mine that
are lying about. Here you are, have

E

them. I can't play alone. They are
getting dirty and are of no use to me.

Boys

How jolly ! What fine toys ! Look,
here's a ship. There's old mother
Jatai. Isn't this a gorgeous sepoy ?
And you'll let us have them all ?
You don't really mind ?

Amal

No, not a bit ; have them by all
means.

A Boy

You don't want them back ?

Amal

Oh, no, I shan't want them.

A Boy

Say, won't you get a scolding for
this ?

Amal

No one will scold me.   But will you
play with them in front of our door
for a while every morning ?   I'll get
you new ones when these are old.

A Boy

Oh, yes, we will.   I say, put these
sepoys into a line.   We'll play at
war ; where can we get a musket ?
Oh, look here, this bit of reed will do
nicely.   Say, but you're off to sleep
already.

Amal

I'm afraid I'm sleepy.   I don't know,
I feel like it at times.   I have been
sitting a long while and I'm tired ;
my back aches.

A Boy

It's hardly mid-day now.   How is it
you're sleepy ?   Listen !   The gong's
sounding the first watch.

Amal

Yes, dong, dong, dong, it tolls me to sleep.

A Boy

We had better go then.   We'll come in again to-morrow morning.

Amal

I want to ask you something before you go.   You are always out—do you know of the King's postmen ?

Boys

Yes, quite well.

Amal

Who are they ?   Tell me their names.

A Boy

One's Badal.

Another Boy

Another's Sarat.

Another Boy

There's so many of them.

Amal

Do you think they will know me if there's a letter for me ?

A Boy

Surely, if your name's on the letter they will find you out.

Amal

When you call in to-morrow morning, will you bring one of them along so that he'll know me ?

A Boy

Yes, if you like.

CURTAIN

THE POST OFFICE

ACT II

ACT II

(Amal in Bed.)

Amal

Can't I go near the window to-day, Uncle ? Would the doctor mind that too ?

Madhav

Yes, darling, you see you've made yourself worse squatting there day after day.

Amal

Oh, no, I don't know if it's made me more ill, but I always feel well when I'm there.

Madhav

No, you don't; you squat there
and make friends with the whole lot
of people round here, old and young,
as if they are holding a fair right
under my eaves—flesh and blood won't
stand that strain. Just see—your face
is quite pale.

Amal

Uncle, I fear my fakir 'll pass and
not see me by the window.

Madhav

Your fakir, whoever's that ?

Amal

He comes and chats to me of the
many lands where he's been. I love
to hear him.

Madhav

How's that ? I don't know of any fakirs.

Amal

This is about the time he comes in. I beg of you, by your dear feet, ask him in for a moment to talk to me here.

(*Gaffer enters in a Fakir's Guise.*)

Amal

There you are. Come here, Fakir, by my bedside.

Madhav

Upon my word, but this is——

Gaffer (*winking hard*)

I am the Fakir.

Madhav

It beats my reckoning what you're not.

Amal

Where have you been this time, Fakir ?

Fakir

To the Isle of Parrots. I am just back.

Madhav

The Parrots' Isle !

Fakir

Is it so very astonishing ? I am not like you. A journey doesn't cost a thing. I tramp just where I like.

Amal (clapping)

How jolly for you ! Remember your promise to take me with you as your follower when I'm well.

Fakir

Of course, and I'll teach you so many travellers' secrets that nothing in sea or forest or mountain can bar your way.

Madhav

What's all this rigmarole ?

Gaffer

Amal, my dear, I bow to nothing in sea or mountain ; but if the doctor joins in with this uncle of yours, then I with all my magic must own myself beaten.

Amal

No. Uncle won't tell the doctor. And I promise to lie quiet ; but the day I am well, off I go with the Fakir, and nothing in sea or mountain or torrent shall stand in my way.

Madhav

Fie, dear child, don't keep on harping upon going ! It makes me so sad to hear you talk so.

Amal

Tell me, Fakir, what the Parrots' Isle is like.

Gaffer

It's a land of wonders; it's a haunt of birds. No men are there; and they neither speak nor walk, they simply sing and they fly.

Amal

How glorious! And it's by some sea?

Gaffer

Of course. It's on the sea.

Amal

And green hills are there?

Gaffer

Indeed, they live among the green hills; and in the time of the sunset when there is a red glow on the hillside, all the birds with their green wings go flocking to their nests.

Amal

And there are waterfalls !

Gaffer

Dear me, of course; you don't have a hill without its waterfalls. Oh, it's like molten diamonds; and, my dear, what dances they have! Don't they make the pebbles sing as they rush over them to the sea. No devil of a doctor can stop them for a moment. The birds looked upon me as nothing but a man, merely a trifling creature without wings — and they would have nothing to do with me. Were it not so I would build a small cabin for myself among their crowd of nests and pass my days counting the sea waves.

Amal

How I wish I were a bird! Then——

Gaffer

But that would have been a bit of a job; I hear you've fixed up with the dairyman to be a hawker of curds when you grow up; I'm afraid such business won't flourish among birds; you might land yourself into serious loss.

Madhav

Really this is too much. Between you two I shall turn crazy. Now, I'm off.

Amal

Has the dairyman been, Uncle?

Madhav

And why shouldn't he? He won't bother his head running errands for your pet fakir, in and out among the ne3ts in his Parrots' Isle. But he has left a jar of curds for you saying that he is busy with his niece's wedding in the village, and has to order a band at Kamlipara. ✔

Amal

But he is going to marry me to his little niece.

Gaffer

Dear me, we are in a fix now.

Amal

He said she would be my lovely little bride with a pair of pearl drops in her ears and dressed in a lovely red *saree*; and in the morning she would milk with her own hands the black cow and feed me with warm milk with foam on it from a brand new earthen cruse; and in the evenings she would carry the lamp round the

F

cow-house, and then come and sit by
me to tell me tales of Champa and his
six brothers.

Gaffer

How charming ! It would even
tempt me, a hermit ! But never
mind, dear, about this wedding. Let
it be.   I tell you that when you
marry there'll be no lack of nieces in
his household.

Madhav

Shut up ! This is more than I can
stand.   [*Exit.*

Amal

Fakir, now that Uncle's off, just
tell me, has the King sent me a letter
to the Post Office ?

Gaffer

I gather that his letter has already
started ; it is on the way here.

Amal

On the way ? Where is it ? Is it
on that road winding through the
trees which you can follow to the end
of the forest when the sky is quite
clear after rain ?

Gaffer

That is where it is. You know all
about it already.

Amal

I do, everything.

Gaffer

So I see, but how ?

Amal

I can't say ; but it's quite clear to
me. I fancy I've seen it often in
days long gone by. How long ago
I can't tell. Do you know when ?

I can see it all : there, the King's
postman coming down the hillside
alone, a lantern in his left hand and
on his back a bag of letters ; climbing
down for ever so long, for days and
nights, and where at the foot of the
mountain the waterfall becomes a
stream he takes to the footpath on
the bank and walks on through the
rye ; then comes the sugarcane field
and he disappears into the narrow
lane cutting through the tall stems
of sugarcanes ; then he reaches the
open meadow where the cricket chirps
and where there is not a single man to
be seen, only the snipe wagging their
tails and poking at the mud with
their bills. I can feel him coming
nearer and nearer and my heart becomes glad.

Gaffer

My eyes are not young ; but you
make me see all the same.

Amal

Say, Fakir, do you know the King
who has this Post Office ?

Gaffer

I do ; I go to him for my alms
every day.

Amal

Good ! When I get well, I must
have my alms too from him, mayn't
I ?

Gaffer

You won't need to ask, my dear,
he'll give it to you of his own accord.

Amal

No, I will go to his gate and cry,
" Victory to thee, O King ! " and
dancing to the tabor's sound, ask for
alms. Won't it be nice ?

Gaffer

It will be splendid, and if you're with me, I shall have my full share. But what will you ask ?

Amal

I shall say, " Make me your postman, that I may go about, lantern in hand, delivering your letters from door to door. Don't let me stay at home all day ! "

Gaffer

What is there to be sad for, my child, even were you to stay at home ?

Amal

It isn't sad. When they shut me in here first I felt the day was so long. Since the King's Post Office was put there I like more and more being indoors, and as I think I shall get a letter one day, I feel quite happy and

then I don't mind being quiet and
alone. I wonder if I shall make out
what 'll be in the King's letter ?

Gaffer

Even if you didn't wouldn't it be
enough if it just bore your name ?

(*Madhav enters.*)

Madhav

Have you any idea of the trouble
you've got me into, between you two ?

Gaffer

What's the matter ?

Madhav

I hear you've let it get rumoured
about that the King has planted his
office here to send messages to both
of you.

Gaffer

Well, what about it ?

Madhav

Our headman Panchanan has had it told to the King anonymously.

Gaffer

Aren't we aware that everything reaches the King's ears ?

Madhav

Then why don't you look out ? Why take the King's name in vain ? You'll bring me to ruin if you do.

Amal

Say, Fakir, will the King be cross ?

Gaffer

Cross, nonsense ! And with a child like you and a fakir such as I am.

let's see if the King be angry, and then won't I give him a piece of my mind.

Amal

Say, Fakir, I've been feeling a sort of darkness coming over my eyes since the morning. Everything seems like a dream. I long to be quiet. I don't feel like talking at all. Won't the King's letter come? Suppose this room melts away all on a sudden, suppose——

Gaffer (*fanning Amal*)

The letter's sure to come to-day, my boy.

(*Doctor enters.*)

Doctor

And how do you feel to-day?

Amal

Feel awfully well to-day, Doctor.
All pain seems to have left me.

Doctor (aside to Madhav)

Don't quite like the look of that
smile. Bad sign that, his feeling well !
Chakradhan has observed——

Madhav

For goodness' sake, Doctor, leave
Chakradhan alone. Tell me what's
going to happen ?

Doctor

Can't hold him in much longer, I
fear ! I warned you before — this
looks like a fresh exposure.

Madhav

No, I've used the utmost care,
never let him out of doors ; and the
windows have been shut almost all
the time.

Doctor

There's a peculiar quality in the
air to-day. As I came in I found
a fearful draught through your front
door. That's most hurtful. Better
lock it at once. Would it matter if
this kept your visitors off for two or
three days ? If some one happens to
call unexpectedly—there's the back
door. You had better shut this window
as well, it's letting in the sunset rays
only to keep the patient awake.

Madhav

Amal has shut his eyes. I expect
he is sleeping. His face tells me—
Oh, Doctor, I bring in a child who is
a stranger and love him as my own,
and now I suppose I must lose him !

Doctor

What's that ? There's your headman sailing in !—What a bother ! I

must be going, brother. You had
better stir about and see to the doors
being properly fastened. I will send
on a strong dose directly I get home.
Try it on him—it may save him at
last, if he can be saved at all.

[*Exeunt Madhav and Doctor.*

(*The Headman enters.*)

Headman

Hello, urchin !——

Gaffer (*rising hastily*)

'Sh, be quiet.

Amal

No, Fakir, did you think I was
asleep ? I wasn't. I can hear everything ; yes, and voices far away. I
feel that mother and father are sitting
by my pillow and speaking to me.

(*Madhav enters.*)

Headman

I say, Madhav, I hear you hobnob
with bigwigs nowadays.

Madhav

Spare me your jokes, Headman, we
are but common people.

Headman

But your child here is expecting a
letter from the King.

Madhav

Don't you take any notice of him,
a mere foolish boy !

Headman

Indeed, why not ! It'll beat the
King hard to find a better family !
Don't you see why the King plants
his new Post Office right before your
window ? Why, there's a letter for
you from the King, urchin.

Amal (starting up)

Indeed, really !

Headman

How can it be false ? You're
the King's chum. Here's your letter
(*showing a blank slip of paper*). Ha,
ha, ha ! This is the letter.

Amal

Please don't mock me. Say, Fakir,
is it so ?

Gaffer

Yes, my dear. I as Fakir tell you
it *is* his letter.

Amal

How is it I can't see ? It all looks
so blank to me. What is there in
the letter, Mr. Headman ?

Headman

The King says, " I am calling on you shortly; you had better have puffed rice for me. — Palace fare is quite tasteless to me now." Ha! ha! ha !

Madhav (*with folded palms*)

I beseech you, Headman, don't you joke about these things——

Gaffer

Joking indeed! He would not dare.

Madhav

Are you out of your mind too, Gaffer ?

Gaffer

Out of my mind, well then I am ; I can read plainly that the King writes he will come himself to see Amal, with the State Physician.

Amal

Fakir, Fakir, 'sh, his trumpet! Can't you hear?

Headman

Ha! ha! ha! I fear he won't until he's a bit more off his head.

Amal

Mr. Headman, I thought you were cross with me and didn't love me. I never could have believed you would fetch me the King's letter. Let me wipe the dust off your feet.

Headman

This little child does have an instinct of reverence. Though a little silly, he has a good heart.

Amal

It's hard on the fourth watch now, I suppose—Hark the gong, " Dong,

dong, ding — Dong, dong, ding." Is
the evening star up ? How is it I
can't see——

Gaffer

Oh, the windows are all shut, I'll
open them.

(*A knocking outside.*)

Madhav

What's that ?—Who is it ?—What a
bother !

Voice (*from outside*)

Open the door.

Madhav

Headman — I hope they're not
robbers.

Headman

Who's there ?—It is Panchanan,
the headman, who calls.—Aren't you

G

afraid to make that noise ?   Fancy !
The noise has ceased ! Panchanan's
voice carries far.—Yes, show me the
biggest robbers !——

Madhav (peering out of the window)

No wonder the noise has ceased.
They've smashed the outer door.

(*The King's Herald enters.*)

Herald

Our Sovereign King comes to-night !

Headman

My God !

Amal

At what hour of the night, Herald ?

Herald

On the second watch.

Amal

When my friend the watchman will strike his gong from the city gates, " ding dong ding, ding dong ding "— then ?

Herald

Yes, then. The King sends his greatest physician to attend on his young friend.

(*State Physician enters.*)

State Physician

What's this ? How close it is here ! Open wide all the doors and windows. (*Feeling Amal's body.*) How do you feel, my child ?

Amal

I feel very well, Doctor, very well. All pain is gone. How fresh and open ! I can see all the stars now twinkling from the other side of the dark.

Physician

Will you feel well enough to leave your bed when the King comes in the middle watches of the night?

Amal

Of course, I'm dying to be about for ever so long. I'll ask the King to find me the polar star.—I must have seen it often, but I don't know exactly which it is.

Physician

He will tell you everything. (*To Madhav.*) Arrange flowers through the room for the King's visit? (*Indicating the Headman.*) We can't have that person in here.

Amal

No, let him be, Doctor. He is a friend. It was he who brought me the King's letter.

Physician

Very well, my child. He may remain if he is a friend of yours.

Madhav (whispering into Amal's ear)

My child, the King loves you. He is coming himself. Beg for a gift from him. You know our humble circumstances.

Amal

Don't you worry, Uncle.—I've made up my mind about it.

Madhav

What is it, my child ?

Amal

I shall ask him to make me one of his postmen that I may wander far and wide, delivering his message from door to door.

Madhav (slapping his forehead)
Alas, is that all ?

Amal
What 'll be our offerings to the
King, Uncle, when he comes ?

Herald
He has commanded puffed rice.

Amal
Puffed rice !   Say, Headman, you're
right. You said so. You knew all
we didn't.

Headman
If you would send word to my
house I could manage for the King's
advent really nice——

Physician
No need at all. Now be quiet all
of you. Sleep is coming over him.
I'll sit by his pillow ; he's dropping

asleep. Blow out the oil-lamp. Only
let the star-light stream in. Hush, he
sleeps.

Madhav (addressing Gaffer)

What are you standing there for
like a statue, folding your palms ?—
I am nervous.—Say, are there good
omens ? Why are they darkening the
room ? How will star-light help ?

Gaffer

Silence, unbeliever.

(Sudha enters.)

Sudha

Amal !

Physician

He's asleep.

Sudha

· I have some flowers for him. Mayn't
I give them into his own hand ?

Physician

Yes, you may.

Sudha

When will he be awake ?

Physician

Directly the King comes and calls him.

Sudha

Will you whisper a word for me in his ear ?

Physician

What shall I say ?

Sudha

Tell him Sudha has not forgotten him.

CURTAIN.

Printed by R. & R. CLARK, LIMITED, *Edinburgh.*

Printed in the United States
82877LV00002B/1/A